T0196466

Waiting for Music in Woody Point

Tony Payne

authorHOUSE®

AuthorHouse™
1663 Liberty Drive
Bloomington, IN 47403
www.authorhouse.com
Phone: 1 (800) 839-8640

Published by AuthorHouse   12/22/2015

ISBN: 978-1-5049-7021-1 (sc)
ISBN: 978-1-5049-7022-8 (e)

Waiting For Music in Woody Point
Written by Tony Hillyard Payne
P.O. Box 183
Bonne Bay, Newfoundland, Canada
Phone 709-458-8887
Email tonyhpayne@hotmail.ca

waiting for music

If you know how to play the fiddle
Or make music with your old guitar
Don't be afraid to share your talent
Sit down right where you are

I have been writing lyrics
Without music to make you dance
Just a few rhymes scribbled on paper
Feel free to take a chance

I don't care if it is easy listening
I don't care if it is rock and roll
If you can write country music
It will be good for my country soul

I write at least a song a day
365 of them can't be bad
You can choose the happy tunes
Or you can choose the ones that's sad

And if you have some time to teach me
A chord or two would be fine
You may need a little patience
Maybe I could make some music mine

So take your time and read each page
You're sure to find at least one you like
I promise not to sing to loud
For fear some will take my mike

Tony Payne 2015-1

1

Lonely Makes the Best Melodies

Sitting all alone here with shadows
Seems no one talks to me at all
I'm just thinking about some old friends
With the clock ticking on the wall

I can't say that I'm not grateful
For all life as given me
But sometimes I need this lonely feeling
Because lonely makes the best melodies

Sometimes I think I can hear my heart beat
I feel the message that it's sending around
I'm sure there is a reason god as made me lonesome
And keep my feet standing on the ground

As I look out through my window
I see all the dark clouds disappear
I look forward to a brighter future with sunshine
As happy visons become more clear

I can't say that I'm not grateful
For all life as given me
But sometimes I need this lonely feeling
Because lonely makes the best melodies

Tony Payne 2015-2

Still Haven't Loved Enough

I see my kids out playing in the yard
I hear everything they say
They know how much I love them
No one knows how much I pray

So many things that I have done
You would think that I would be tough
I smoked too much, toked too much, and drank too much
But I still haven't loved enough

The kids all keep me grounded
To this place that I call home
Each one can find their solace
If ever they get the need to roam

I still have lots of love to give
My heart is still right full
I think with each act of love I give
More returns, it is the loving rule

So many things that I have done
You would think that I would be tough
I smoked too much, toked too much, and drank too much
But I still haven't loved enough

I wish I could change the people
To see this priceless world we live in
Sharing peace and love forever
Our kids could live happy without much sin

I'm going to live forever
Through everything they do
My hope that everyone finds true love
In themselves and others too!

So many things that I have done
You would think that I would be tough
I smoked too much, toked too much, and drank too much
But I still haven't loved enough

Tony Payne 2015-3

when the stones have fallen down

We will still hear Mick Jagger
When the stones have fallen down
Music just lives forever
Even inside a dying town

Music as a way to calm us
Everyone sings that I know
Some are better than others
Music gets us in that magic glow

Perhaps we can go out dancing
With some friends that are real loud
We can scream and shout
Singing high when we are in the crowd

When the music finally hits you
You feel the passion come alive
It happens if you are out dancing
Or in the country for a romantic drive

If all our kids were taught music
Where they could feel the passion when they sing
Our whole wide world would be smiling
We would be amazed at the happiness it brings

We will still hear Mick Jagger
When the stones have fallen down
Music just lives on forever
Even inside a dying town

Tony Payne 2015-4

Is She a Good Woman?

I just watched her walk, right a pass me down the street
She looked like someone, I would really like to meet
But how can you tell, with just a glance along the way
Was it true love that walked by today

Is she a good woman because she's a blonde with blue eyes
Is her heart bitter because of some other man's lies
Will she be happy just because she is pretty
Will she love your kids, or want you to move to the city

You can never tell by the way that they walk
She won't fall in love because of the way that you talk
You can never tell, if with your kids she will play
What can you go by, but the things she might say

You're scared to get close to a woman so fine
You're scared you will love her, and she'll make you blind
Your kids need protection, they deserve the best
You have been hurt before, but you must never confess

Is she a good woman because she's a blonde with blue eyes
Is her heart bitter because of some other man's lies
Will she be happy just because she is pretty
Will she love your kids, or want you to move to the city

Take your time slow, don't jump to fast
Make sure you are ready, be content with your past
Treat everyone nice, and you'll surely find
A great woman to love you, you won't be left behind

Open your heart up, let love find a way in
Don't hate everyone, before you begin
In order to love, first you must trust
But you have to be willing, that is a must

Is she a good woman because she's a blonde with blue eyes
Is her heart bitter because of some other man's lies
Will she be happy just because she is pretty
Will she love your kids, or want you to move to the city

Tony Payne 2015-5

I Won't Chase You Any More

I used to chase the women, and buy them drinks out at the bar
With hopes to go out dating, that never got me very far
I used to think that money, could buy everything I need
Love, peace, and wisdom, I didn't want any weed

I used to love to go out dancing, you couldn't get me off the floor
Drink myself into a happy stupor, stay out each night until four
Everyone would be your friend, right up until closing time
Then I'd find myself alone, even with a woman by my side

I still love to have a drink, but it's not the same
Buying a ladies friendship, so I could find one to claim
I have become more content alone, watching everything they do
I won't chase a pretty face any more, to be with an insecure you

If you see me at the bar, standing all alone
I won't give no guarantee that I'm not whiskey stoned
But don't think that I lost interest, with the ladies on the floor
I will gladly talk to one, but I won't chase you any more
So if you think I'm desolate, when I walk alone out through the door
You may have read me all wrong, I'm not lonely like before
If you want to talk to me, I will try not to get you bored
I hope we can find some common interest, but I won't chase you anymore

Tony Payne 2015 -6

I Think Jesus Looked Away

I've loved more than my share
And I've had my ins and outs
I've always believed in Heaven
Even though I've had my doubts

I always tried to do my best
With mistakes I dare not say
I always asked Jesus for forgiveness
I think this time he looked away

I've been alone for some time now
I knew I would have to pay the piper
There are lots of things I should not have done
But baby you know I ain't no viper

I can't dance
And I can't sing
I won't fight
Or do bad things
I will treat you right
And I won't bring you shame
I can love you honey
Can you give me the same

I always tried to do my best
With mistakes I dare not say
I always asked Jesus for forgiveness
I think this time he looked away

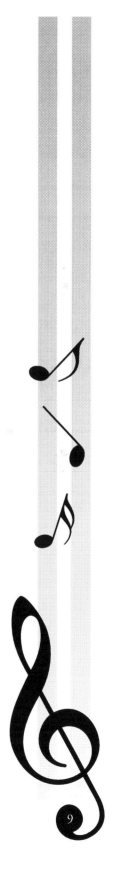

9

I don't believe in religion
But I believe in a higher power
If you believe in me girl
Let's stand in the midnight hour

I won't make no promises
I don't plan to keep
I hope I make you happy
So you can trust me in your sleep

I won't ask the lord for forgiveness
Cause I don't believe in him any more
I'm on a higher level
Than I ever been before

I've already forgiven me
For things I may have done
Let's walk up on the sandy beach
And you and I soak up the sun.

I always tried to do my best
With mistakes I dare not say
I always asked Jesus for forgiveness
I think this time he looked away

Tony Payne 2015-7

In The Morning

The first time that I saw her
She was dancing with such grace
She stopped and walked toward me
I could see a lovely smile on her face

She stopped and asked me for a light
I told her she could spend the night
With an old drunk that don't drink no more
But I had lots to offer her for sure

I offered her a flickered flame
She held my hands as if by shame
I had my dreams, my hopes too
A pretty face and eyes of blue

She stayed in my arms
All night long
We made love
To every song
But in the morning she was gone
Yes in the morning she was gone

Tony Payne 2015-8

Looking For a Peaceful Man

Time it passes on, even when you are asleep
Sometimes you're just so lonely, because of the company you keep
Most times when you're flying solo, and thinking is all you do
You don't want a drink, but you need something to get you through

You want to leave this life, and go walking through the trees
Sailing on the sunset, or on a beach with a calming breeze
Sometimes you want to go away, and be able to not look back
I've done my share of thinking, I made what was white looked black

Riding through the desert,
On a white horse in the sand
When you're looking for your soul
When you're looking for a peaceful man

Running aint the answer, you have to face the pain
You have to take your chances, even though it may happen all again
You look for all the questions, for the answers that you seek
Everything drives you crazy, and drinking makes you weak

You just keep on hiding, behind your smiling face
No one feels your pain, which never leaves your place
You just go on searching, through the darkness for the light
You are hoping for forgiveness, somewhere in the night

12

Riding through the desert,
On a white horse in the sand
When you're looking for your soul
When you're looking for a peaceful man

You are feeling all alone, your friends a but a few
Old ones are all gone, seems you have to pay for any new
You just go on searching, for the man you want to be
You may find forgiveness, and your conscience will set you free

Riding through the desert,
On a white horse in the sand
When you're looking for your soul
When you're looking for a peaceful man

Tony Payne 2015-9

To The Devil and The Cross

I went looking for myself, in the bottom of a glass
What I found was emptiness, returning from the past
I tried to find my soul, in a bible that I found
But the words that I read, couldn't keep me from being down

I wish I had a good thought,
For everting I think I lost
For every time I sold my soul
To the devil or for the cross

I kept looking in the wrong places,
To find the peace I was looking for
In the house of insecurities,
From drunks with self-made wars

Maybe in a boat out on the ocean
My soul it would feel clean
Or by myself upon a mountain top
I could close my eyes and dream
I wish I had a good thought,
For everting I think I lost
For every time I sold my soul
To the devil or for the cross

Someday when I find peace
I know I will find love inside of me
Maybe I should climb that mountain
And start really being free.

Tony Payne 2015-10

14

Weathered and Rusty

I've been lonely for so long
Wondering where it is that I went wrong
Always singing that same old song
Looking out at the dark cloudy day

No one to help me fail or try
No one to see me when I cry
I have no reason now to lie
Hoping for warm winds in May

My car is getting weathered and rusty
My face as become wrinkled and crusty
My mind is beaten it's no longer trusty
And they say I'm getting old

They have taken all I had
My kids are living without their dad
Sometimes I get feeling really sad
And I feel like a ship that sunk
Well I ain't ready for no old age home
I can still fight when I'm not stoned
I think too much when I'm alone
I can still make love when I'm not too drunk

My car is getting weathered and rusty
My face as become wrinkled and crusty
My mind is beaten it's no longer trusty
And they say I'm getting old

Tony Payne 2015-11

Too Easy When I'm Stoned

I was standing toking on the corner
When an old man came up to me
He said "let me tell you something son
That stuff will never set you free"

You get too angry when you're lonely
Too easy when you're stoned
And you're consumed with emptiness
When you find yourself alone

Looking in the bottom of a bottle
For a friend you hope you find
Then one day you look into a looking glass
At the wrinkles from the wine

Your wife as gone and left you
And your kids gave up as well
You may even look real happy
But its only you can tell
You no longer ask the lord for anything
Or thank him for your soul
You're just hoping that you die
Before you get too old

You get too angry when you're lonely
Too easy when you're stoned
And you're consumed with emptiness
When you find yourself alone

Then he turned and walked away
Not wanting no reply
I threw away my case of emptiness
And went inside the church to ask god why

I didn't hear any answers
He never gave me a place to hide
It wasn't long before I realized
Heaven and hell is a place inside

The path of least resistance
Is the only path to take
I can come to love myself
Without one ounce of pride to shake

All your friends have abandoned you
You hear the voices say
You start to believe they have no time
But you're the one that walked away

I get too angry when I'm lonely
I'm too easy when I'm stoned
And I'm consumed with emptiness
When I find myself alone

Tony Payne 2015-12

A pretty Face

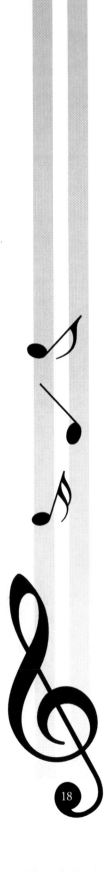

You can put a fancy smile
Upon a pretty face
You can have all kinds of money
So material things can be replaced

People think you are doing well
You have adjusted to impress
Most people will always judge you
On how well you learn to dress

Hardly anyone looks into your eyes
To see what you hide inside
You can go out window shopping
And ask her to be your bride

You think that because you have the world
To do just as you please
But if you're not content and happy
It will bring you to your knees
There are things that are worse than dying
When your mind is maimed
You can always pretend for others
Even though your soul is drained

You can be sad forever
You can hide it all away
But if you don't find contentment
It's only you who will have to pay.

Tony Payne 2015-13

The Old Man

He had a pretty picture, of his family on the wall
He was selling all his dreams of yesterday
He couldn't look any richer, even though they never call
The price of a bottle, I'd have to pay

I picked up a baseball glove and handed him some cash
He took it, but a tear came to his eye
I asked him what's the matter, even though it looked like trash
He said it was his sons, when he was young and shy

He offered me a chair, and a full glass of lonely
And said won't you join me for a yarn
I used to be so happy, I wasn't always phoney
And this place didn't always look like a fragging barn

I'm a drunk, I'm a coward, and I'm going home tomorrow
I'm a stoner and an addict and I have nothing else to do
I had my wife here with me, I just brought her sorrow
I wish I could have helped her, and it breaks my heart into
I sat and listened for a while, to an old drunk looking for pity
He was making excuses for his luck that I thought was a lie
My job is not fulfilling, and I can't stand this city
But I guess I'm stuck here until I die

I said thank you for the drink, as I finished my last drop
I did not understand just what he tried to say to me
He said thank you for listening. And I hope you don't forget
The next day I read the paper, it simply said they found that old man hanging from a tree.

I'm a drunk, I'm a coward, and I'm going home tomorrow
I'm a stoner and an addict and I have nothing else to do
I had my wife here with me, I just brought her sorrow
I wish I could have helped her, and it breaks my heart into

Tony Payne 2015-14

I could sense the devil from the wine

I met up with a lady, I asked if she would like a drink
She said thank you mister, and gave me a little wink
As we talked the night away, I knew that I was done
I asked if she would like a drink, she said "yes" with a forked tongue

Humility is the only thing, which makes angles out of men
As she held me close, I knew I couldn't win
Pride makes angles into devils, I was no longer blind
As she held onto my hand, I could sense the devil from the wine

As we danced into the night, I felt an angle by my side
Because of loneliness and emptiness, a had no place to hide
We drank a bottle of insecurity, as Satan showed her face
I could feel it warming up in a forbidden place

She took me back to her den, I remember crosses on the wall
I felt as I slipped inside, I thought she is not bad at all
I remember sleeping with an angle, as we made love that night
I woke up with a tainted heart, to Lucifer's delight

Humility is the only thing, which makes angles out of men
As she held me close, I knew I couldn't win
Pride makes angles into devils, I was no longer blind
As she held onto my hand, I could sense the devil from the wine

Let me say once you get inside, you may never find the key
What once was warm, turns to ice, and you will never be set free
There is a place called heaven, where everyone lives quite well
But if you're still dancing with the devil, you will always live in hell.

Humility is the only thing, which makes angles out of men
As she held me close, I knew I couldn't win
Pride makes angles into devils, I was no longer blind
As she held onto my hand, I could sense the devil from the wine

Tony Payne2015-15

20

Let's pretend

Let's pretend that we are happy
And go out to the dance
Let's pretend that we love each other
People will think we have a chance

Maybe by the time the night is over
We will be too drunk to tell
And we can make love together
Without feeling like we belong in hell

Maybe after a drink or two
You can stand to talk to me
Or maybe you can spell you guts
To others who are pretending to be free

I won't mind to hold you close
Like you're the only one
I can even smile at you
And pretend we're having fun
If you should get drunk enough
To say I love you
Maybe I will believe
All the words are true

Or perhaps I will stay sober
And stay your faithful ride
But if you want to make love all night
Some feelings I just can't hide.

Tony Payne 2015-16

No Matter What the Weather

I've lived a life of loneliness
Never thinking I would grow old
I've felt the feeling of emptiness
Just wanting the devil to take my soul

I've hidden on the inside of a bottle
Working toward the bottom
When my faith has been abandoned
And my beliefs have gotten rotten

I've smoked weed all by my lonesome
While sitting on a mountain top
Thinking of jumping over
Never knowing what made me stop

I've stood inside a bar with a glass of emptiness
With a thousand people around
Never been so alone
And hopping that I drown

I've lived a life of loneliness
Never thinking I would grow old
I've felt the feeling of emptiness
Just wanting the devil to take my soul

I've done a lot of reading
About my lonely and my bleeding
And the only thing I find
Is the pain I've created with my mind

Now I look out through the window
Where the sun is always shining
No matter what the weather
It will be lonely if you're whining

Tony Payne 2015-17

22

Second Hand Wife

I was thinking about things
Just the other day
What I thought was love
Sort of fades away

I'm getting older
And now I'm alone
Should I stay single
Or pick up the phone

Am I getting too old
To be enjoying my life
Should I buy a new car
Or a second hand wife

In five years you know
With a new car I'm free
But if I sign those papers
It will take the good out of me
The car will never get jealous
If you glance at a car that is red
But a second hand heart
Will accuse you of trying to take her to bed

Am I getting too old
To be enjoying my life
Should I buy a new car
Or a second hand wife

The old car may get rusty
But you can sell it for parts
The other gets fussy
And won't shut up once she starts

Am I getting too old
To be enjoying my life
Should I buy a new car
Or a second hand wife

Tony Payne 2015-18

24

The Frump

I was walking down on Main Street
Pretty girls were walking by
They were all in such a hurry
Like an alcoholic for the rye

Then I saw a lady sitting
Looked like she hadn't washed for years
Was it a fuddy duddy dowdy frump
With a hiatus between her hears

I thought she would ask me for a dollar
When she spoke to me
But when I got to her ragged spot
She said won't you join me for a tea

She took me by great surprize
I didn't know what to say
So I knelt down right beside her
And asked how much I would have to pay
She said my son I'm not that poor
I have all the processions that I need
And if you sit with me a while
You may forget your heart of greed

You see I once wore pearls
And had a silken dress
I could walk by any man
Who needed to be impressed

But there was always something missing
From my lonely heart
I never had any children
And that just tore me right apart

25

I never got to find true love
That only children bring
Then I saw a starving child
And I sold my wedding ring

My life it must have turned around
When most people thought I was poor
To see the kids eyes light up for a hug
I was way richer than before

So please sir, don't judge others
And enjoy your cup of tea
I have no processions left
And I'm as happy as could be

I think I felt a load left
As I finished my last drop
I realized how selfish I have been
And was really glad I stopped

She gently squeezed my trembling hand
And said don't worry son
When you give back to the world
You will know your war is won

So if you see a dowdy frump
She may not have a hiatus between her ears
Stop and be enlightened
You may shed some happy tears

Some of the riches people around
Don't have a penny to call their own
Let your heart feel the happiness
And you will never feel alone

Tony Payne 2015-19

when the darkness disappears

If your world seems dark and dreary
And you're wanting to get stoned
If you want to see more clearly
When you wake up all alone

Everyone is in a panic
And you don't know who to trust
The government is creating wars
And the people are quite quick to adjust

The police don't need a reason
To arrest you anymore
Our leaders are all happy
As long as we are at war

Now if you dream of changes
From always being in fear
Everything will be brighter
When the darkness disappears
The churches are all corrupt
They make you lose your faith in god
How the hell can you ever know
If Jesus was a fraud

Love is the only thing
That makes you feel real great
But when it comes to women
You usually end up late

Now if you dream of changes
From always being in fear
Everything will be brighter
When the darkness disappears

It seems that you are scared to death
That you will end up as one
Nothing makes you happy
And you walk away from fun

You walk into a church
For a religion you have no like
But you won't step behind the alter
For fear of a lightning strike

As light is the only thing
That can make darkness dissipate
When you come to love yourself
The world will know no hate

Now if you dream of changes
From always being in fear
Everything will be brighter
When the darkness disappears

Tony Payne 2015-20

The Devil in Your Head

When you're born feeling lonely
And you grow up drunk and stoney
And the good lord as taken all you got
You're praying for tomorrow
To rid your life of sorrow
And the seeds you sowed as turned to friggin rot

The beer might dull the pain
But the whiskey brings it back again
Where you end up in some stranger's bed
She gives you black coffee with a smoke
You think love is just a joke
Memories bring you back to what the bible said

Ask and you shall receive
Have all you want if you believe
But the devil in your head can cast a curse
You make all kinds of money
And spend it all on milk and honey
Until you wake up with an empty purse

You want to turn your life around
Look for the love you never found
From the inside of your ever aching heart
Your kids don't deserve the anger
When you feel you are in danger
Of a life of hatred that they never played a part

Come in from the lonely cold
Where your soul cannot be sold
To the devil that lives inside your mind
Go out walking amongst big trees
You just may find the beauty to be free
And the happiness that you never thought you'd find

There is a light that shines
Without the whiskey, beer and wine
You can turn it on all you have to do is try
You will find a love that's true
When you lean to loving you
And your soul will live on forever when you die.

Tony Payne 2015-21

For Your Wedding Ring

I hear the phone out there ringing
I was hoping that you would call
Your bath robe is still there
At the end of the cold dark hall

Your necklace it still hangs
Where it used to be
The house it is so lonely
Since it's only me

The keys they are still hanging
For your car out in the drive
I can't say that I miss you
But I hear you're still alive

But just in case you're wondering
I haven't changed a thing
Except there is no finger
For your wedding ring
I talk away to your picture
At least you're smiling there
You never say you hate me
So I guess I you really care

And if you hear I miss you
No one can really know
Everything is still the same
It's like you didn't go

So if you should return
Your keys still fits the door
I will never take you for granted
You won't feel you are always needing more

But just in case you're wondering
I haven't changed a thing
Except there is no finger
For your wedding ring

You pillow hasn't been slept on
Your perfume hasn't been used
I do keep some Vodka now
For when I get the blues

So please don't think I miss you
From how much you hear I drink
You're always on my mind
Whenever I feel the urge to drink

They are saying I still love you
Please don't think I'm missing you at all
But sometimes I hear the phone ringing
When I'm wishing that you call

But just in case you're wondering
I haven't changed a thing
Except there is no finger
For your wedding ring

So if you think that you still need me
Just come right on home
I will stop imagining
That I can hear you on the phone

But just in case you're wondering
I haven't changed a thing
Except there is no finger
For your wedding ring
Except there is no finger
For your wedding ring

Tony Payne 2015-22

32

Long Before My Fall

Listen to the loons out on the bay
And their lonely forlorn call
It reminds me of days gone by
Long before my fall

I see a badly beaten horse
Shortly after it leaves its stall
It tells me of days gone by
Long before my fall

And a baby in its daddy's arms
Wanting to walk before they crawl
I loved how my children held me tight
Long before my fall

I hear every sound this lonesome house makes
I see your picture on the wall
I reminisce about our long lost love
Long before my fall

Tony Payne 2015-23

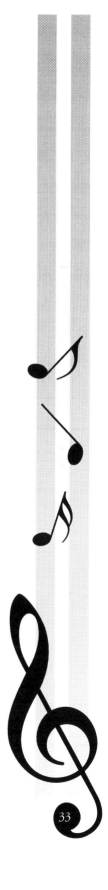

Jesus I Walked alone

I was always told to believe in Jesus
That he died for me on the cross
How was I to know the difference
I never counted every loss

I always had trouble believing in me
And I had the need of getting stoned
When I needed a guiding light
Jesus I walked alone

You see I asked for his forgiveness
For every mistake I made
But I had to learn to forgive myself
Only I know the price I paid

I've learned to hold my head up high
There was no person I could phone
When I dealt with the torment in my soul
Jesus I walked alone
I'm not saying there is no God above
Who created all this beautiful stuff
Like children, flowers, and puppy dogs
But sometimes we don't love our selves enough

I just don't believe in the God almighty
That sits up there on a thrown
When it comes to the love I need
Jesus I walk alone

Tony Payne 2015-24

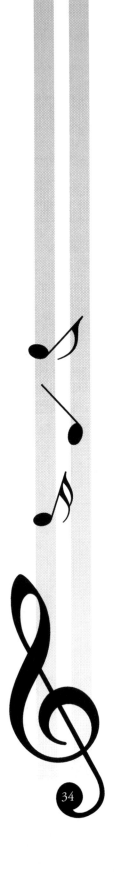

34

I Want To Be a Fisherman

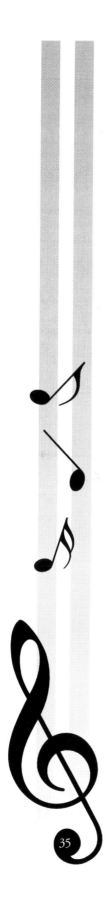

I played a show tonight in Denver
Everyone came out to see
The man, the myth, the legend
Who sang songs of being free

I gave them what they ask for
While most of them were stoned
I took a pretty girl back to my hotel room
But my mind was there alone

She said it must be great to be famous
And to be in a super band
I said I wish I weren't so lonely
Sometimes I wish I were a fisherman

All the people flock around you
But no one cares about your heart
You sing songs of being lonely
But no one sees you fall apart

You have all kinds of money
You can buy fish right in the pan
Sometimes I wish I could start over
And be a fisherman

You talk of being free
You have the money to buy the fans
But I wouldn't be half as lonely
If I were a fisherman

Tony Payne 2015-25

The Last Page

Imagination is more important than knowledge
It can release you from the cage
If I were to write a book of love
Your name would appear on every page

Repetition is the master of all skill
Maybe I can earn an extra wage
So many ways I know I love you
I don't want to save it for the last page

No matter how bad things are
And we go off in a rage
Someone always as it worse than us
No love found before the last page

You know I'm no good at acting
You will never see me lying on a stage
Sometimes you may think that I'm the jester
Just dancing my way unto the last page
Long after we are old and wrinkled
I won't care about our age
I know that I will still love you
Long after you turn the last page

Tony Payne 2015-26

Only The Heart Can See

Sometimes only the heart can see
What is invisible to the naked eye
When you lose true love forever
And I t causes your soul to die

How do I face the world without you
When i know that I can't win
My friends tell me to forget about you
But it's not easy to try again

No one sees me cry at night
For the love I know I lost
There is a price to pay for being alone
I'm not sure it's worth the cost

Since you're not moving on
It don't get any easier for me
I keep thinking you're still hoping
And my love for you just can't be free
In the short time we spent together
In our secret love embrace
You stole my heart for ever
And left me with the pain to face

Sometimes only the heart can see
What is invisible to the naked eye
When you lose true love forever
And I t causes your soul to die

Tony Payne 2015-27

Think It All Away

There's a solution, to every problem
That you encounter, every day
So if you're troubled, by your worries
Put on a smile, and think it all away

The storms of winter, can drive you crazy
There will be no flowers, this coming May
So if your life, is full of storms
Put on some music, and dance it all away

If you gave up, on religion
And to their god, you no longer pray
Set your sites, on higher power
And just think it all away

If you're afraid, about how you live
Because you listen, to what people say
It's up to you, to make you happy
So paint a picture, you won't be grey

Tony Payne 2015 -28

38

I You Don't Love Me

(Man Singing)

If you don't love me, you won't miss me darlin
If you don't love me, you won't really care
If you don't love me, life is not worth living
If you don't love me, let me make it clear

You see I love you, and I miss you darlin
You see I love you, and I really care
You see I love you, you make my life worth living
You see I love you, which is all so clear

(Woman singing)
Will I won't tell you, that I love you darlin
I won't tell you, that I really care
I won't tell you, your life it is worth living
But I will tell you, just so it is clear

I need you, and I miss you darlin
I want you, but I live in fear
I will tell you, please come back tomorrow
Oh darling, I just need you here.

Tony Payne 2015-29

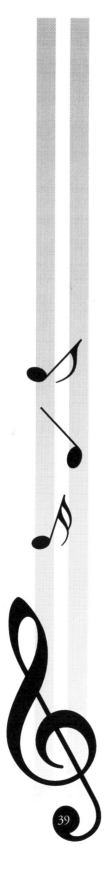

39

whiskey Stoned

I'm heading out to Fort Mac
I wish you could come along
I know it must be lonely
I know leaving you is wrong

I know the hardships of a lady
When you are left home alone
You look for your happiness in a wine bottle
And I get whiskey stoned

Whiskey stoned, all I do is try
Whiskey stoned, when I think about your eyes
You know I love you baby,
But I worry when you cry

Our friends are all breaking up
I was talking to Mick today
He said he is not going home
His best friend Joe took her away

So honey if your heart is breaking
I tell you what I'm gonna do
I don't need a new four wheel drive
But baby I need you

Whiskey stoned, all I do is try
Whiskey stoned, when I think about your eyes
You know I love you baby,
But I worry when you cry

Tony Payne 2015-30

40

Each Night You Keep Me Warm

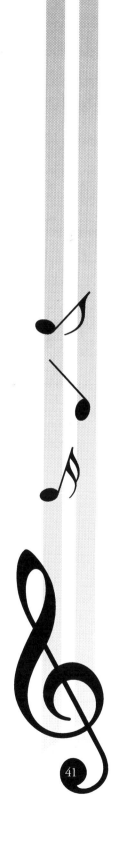

Ever since I saw your face
Standing in the pouring rain
Water running down your face
I could feel your pain

Your eyes looked like an angel
Who just been released from hell
I was hoping I could save you
I did not know you would give me life as well

You are my guiding light
My beacon in the storm
You are the fire in my heart
Each night you keep me warm

I hope you always love me
Like a diamond in the rough
Baby my glass is always full
It's like I always have enough
At times when you hold me close
I know I am a happy man
Our hearts become as one
Like a small bottle of sand

I will love you forever
Long after we are young and bold
Our bodies may show age and wisdom
But our passion will not grow old

You are my guiding light
My beacon in the storm
You are the fire in my heart
Each night you keep me warm

Tony Payne 2015-31

who cares if Others Think You're Strange

Don't worry about who puts you down
Fighting back makes you the clown
Go against the current or you may drown
And live by what you believe

Be very careful about who you trust
Thank the lord, it is a must
Fall for love, but don't fall for lust
Be happy or just leave

Life is too long, to live with hate
If you rely on others, you will have to wait
Will you convince St. Peter at heaven's gate
Or do you believe in hell

If you want to be happy, you're going alone
Moss don't gather on a rolling stone
Inside your mind, you set the tone
Here's to hoping everything goes well
Don't wait for the mountain to come to you
Walk outside and try something new
Care about others, but don't feel blue
And you will see the change

Love yourself and take a chance
Go on a date, don't fear romance
Sing out loud, and have a dance
Who the hell cares who thinks you're strange

Tony Payne 2015-32

You Can't Take It With You

My eyes come open… at 5 am
A chance for freedom… and start again
The sun is rising… over the mountain top
I want to keep climbing… I don't want to stop

So if you see me… out all alone
I'm not lonely… and I'm not stoned
The sites I'm seeing… just blows me away
I'll just use passion… to start my day

You can't take it with you… when you go
Share your passion… let everyone know
Don't keep nothing … on the inside
If you want to be happy… don't run and hide

It seems you're afraid now … don't let things slip by
Love yourself fully… you have to try
You cannot change … the mistakes you made
But you learned real well… from the price you paid
Find true love… with a heart that's free
Keep the love strong… and you will see
Happiness all around you… you won't try to hide
Everything happens … from the inside

You can't take it with you… when you go
Share your passion… let everyone know
Happiness all around you … you won't try and hide
Everything happens… from the inside

Tony Payne 2015-33

43

Love Found

A long time ago, when life was so simple
I fell in love, with a girl oh so sweet
She was so pretty, with the eyes of an angle
The things she did tell me, are my secrets to keep

She was content, to cry on my shoulder
My love for her was all that I knew
We never cared, for the fighting of our parents
We said we'd be together, until we turned 92

We talked of dreams, which only kids know
We lived life so happy, it could never go away
She shared my passion, and we shared our love
Everything was perfect, until that faithful day

I awoke in the morning, to the sound of her crying
Her mom was leaving, for the city you see
I tried to hold her, and said we'd be together
But she wouldn't listen, her mom said they had to break free
I stood there so helpless, because I couldn't hold her
My heart it did break, and the pieces did fall
I was too young, to fight for our love
She left me there crying, and it was great sadness for all

The time passed so slowly, but the years they flew by
My soul it lay empty, waiting for her to return
I looked in the mirror, I saw the face of a stranger
The passion was gone, and the bridges were burned

Then I heard from her family, she was returning
After all this time, she was coming home
I was so happy, when they passed me a hand written letter
But my heart fell cold, when I read "sorry I left you alone"

They said that she died, of being heart broken
She loved me dearly, since the day she had parted
Now my love for her, will go on for ever
And I did what I did, to finish what we had started

I opened a bottle, and took my first sip of whiskey
All that I wanted, was for my sorrows to drown
My love for her, was stronger than freedom
And I didn't stop drinking, until I laid dead on the ground

Please don't feel sorry, for my twist of faith
The drinking didn't kill me, it just took my last breath of life
But now we're together, and we don't have to worry
She was my soulmate, and now in death she is my wife

Tony Payne 2015-34

It Keeps Me from Feeling Blue

I hope you don't think, that I don't hear your talk
About all the things I do
Whenever I see you, I just keep right on walking
It keeps me from feeling blue

Please, don't take this the wrong friggin way
It's none of my business, what you think of me
Friends like you I can do without
I'm quite happy being free

There was a time that all that mattered
Was a smile upon your face
But time as passed, our love is gone
It surely cannot be replaced

It don't seem like I have any friends left
And most times I sleep alone
People ask me if I gave up on love
Because I no longer have the need of getting stoned
Please, don't take this the wrong friggin way
It's none of my business, what you think of me
Friends like you I can do without
I'm quite happy being free

Tony Payne 2015-35

46

I Guess I Miss You Baby

I called in sick today, and headed for my fishing hole
The fish weren't biting much, and I was way too friggin cold
I packed up my fishing tackle, and watched the eagles flying by
My thoughts drifted back to you, had to stop and wonder why

I guess I miss you baby, and the little things you do
I guess I miss you baby, I can't stop loving you

I went on to the bar, to shoot a game of pool
I didn't have to worry, you have the kids and they are still in school
I sat myself down onto a barstool, it's still my favorite place
With every woman's voice I hear, I can see your face

I guess I miss you baby, and the little things you do
I guess I miss you baby, I can't stop loving you

I head on back home at night, the guilt is sitting in
But the fish they may be biting tomorrow, should I try it all again
The boss he may be angry, but do you think I really care
Seems nothing really matters, I still live in fear

I guess I miss you baby, and the little things you do
I guess I miss you baby, I can't stop loving you

Tony Payne 2015-36

47

If I Learn to Play, Sing and Dance

I want to learn to play guitar,
Sing to people near and far
Make people smile, that don't feel on par
Spread peace, love and joy

I can hear the music in my head,
With almost every word that's said
We deserve to laugh, at stupid things we did
And never have to reason why

When I truly learn the beat
I hope that you have to tap your feet
And go dancing out in the street
And use it as your dope

Raise the rhythm way up high
Watch the moon waltz across the sky
Cause some harmony in the great by and by
There will be no need to pray and hope
Music makes us come alive
At a better state we will arrive
Go see a concert, I will drive
There is such a thing as being free

Maybe if I learn to play, sing, and dance
You will join me and take a chance
We can all be happy, if we make a stance
And I wish everyone will sing with me

Tony Payne 2015-37

Sometimes

Sometimes when I close my eyes
And I dream of you
Sometimes late in the night
When there is nothing better to do
Sometimes when the sun don't shine
And the sky is not so blue
I just want to hold your hand
And hope you will hold me too

Sometimes when you walk away
Because of something that I said
Sometimes when you won't talk to me
Because of some stupid thing I did
Sometimes when you put me down
And it fills my heart with dread
I just fall to pieces
And sorrow fills my head

Sometimes when you come to me
You put my heart at ease
Sometimes when you say you love me
I do whatever it is you please
Sometimes late in the night
When all you do is tease
And I know you need me
Like an eagle needs the breeze

Sometimes

Tony Payne 2015-38

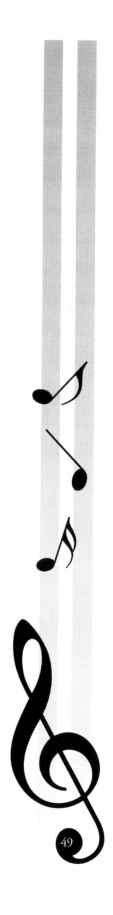

49

Stormy Lonely Night

I'm here listening to the thunder roll
On a rainy night in July
I can't help but worry about you
I remember how it made you cry

The lightning flashes light up the night
I wonder if I should call
I hate to think about you being alone
I wonder if you are alone at all

Baby I sure miss you
On this stormy lonely night
Baby I sure miss you
I pray you're doing alright

As the flashes get close together
I can't get you of my mind
I used to love to hold you
And make love when the darkness made us blind
Now as the night clears
And the storm it do subside
No more rolling thunder
But my heart it still can't hide

Baby I sure miss you
On this stormy lonely night
Baby I sure miss you
I pray you're doing alright

Tony Payne 2015-39

When the Wind Begins To Blow

I can't say I really miss you
The sun is never in the sky
I won't say I want to kiss you
My well is always dry

You won't hear I talked about you
The last time I was drinking rum
Please don't believe I was in fighting order
Because someone called you dumb

The only time I think about you
Is when the wind begins to blow
When the sea is flat calm
Or my darkness begins to show

My friends they talk about you
As if I really care
My momma says I'm lonely
Just because I cry in my beer
My girlfriend says I need you
Because I won't stay the night
And the barmaid tells me to go back to you
When I get in the mood to fight

The only time I think about you
Is when the wind begins to blow
When the sea is flat calm
Or my darkness begins to show

Tony Payne 2015-40

children, Beer and Time?

Listening to my children, playing in the yard
When they come to visit, and bring a Christmas card
No one knows how much you love it, I wish that they could stay
And no one feels the loneliness, when they go away

Nothing can bring happiness
Like smiles, hugs and rhyme
Nothing makes you lonelier
Than children, beer and time

The beer will bring a joyful grin
When they make us laugh when we can't win
Want a friend when we are alone
And make you cry when you can't phone

Nothing can bring happiness
Like smiles, hugs and rhyme
Nothing makes you lonelier
Than children, beer and time
Time is just to make us wise
Gives us freedom without much noise
Cherish our own life with our long- time friends
And leave us alone in the end

Nothing can bring happiness
Like smiles, hugs and rhyme
Nothing makes you lonelier
Than children, beer and time

So when you see your mom and dad
With lots of time to spend with you
Sit right down and enjoy a beer
And have a yarn or two

Nothing can bring happiness
Like smiles, hugs and rhyme
Nothing makes you lonelier
Than children, beer and time

Next time that you turn around
Your children may have moved on
And there is nothing worse than a full case
And no one to urge you to make it gone

Nothing can bring happiness
Like smiles, hugs and rhyme
Nothing makes you lonelier
Than children, beer and time

Tony Payne2015-41

Our Kids Will Learn to Fly

I always hope my children
Can play freely in the street
I hope there is never any danger
From strangers that they meet

I surly the government
Can never take away our right
To speak our mind on anything
Or to stand and fight

I hope my kid's faith is never broken
By people they are taught to trust
Or they never feel the need to sell their soul
For possessions or for lust

A hope they dance and sing with pride
Whenever they feel the need
Where there are no starving children
With hungry mouths to feed

You don't have to look real hard
To see the world is good
We need to teach to give from the heart again
That I know we could

So when you close your eyes at night
Just think of peace and joy
The world will be a better place
And our kids will learn to fly

Tony Payne 2015-42

Summer of 83

Being young, when we knew it all
When our hearts were young and free
No one can take my memories
From the summer of 83

When life gets hard and we have it rough
And people won't let you be
Just sit back and reminisce
About the summer of 83

All your friends have gone and left you
And your wife you no longer see
I think about our first night
In the summer of 83

The radio is playing girly music
That makes no sense to me
I slip on some rock and roll and sing
Just like in the summer of 83

I will always have the good times
To count on one, two, three
I would love to hold you close in my heart
Like I did in the summer of 83

Tony Payne 2015-43

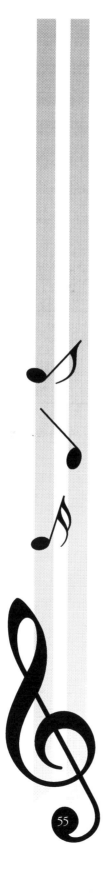

Maybe It's Just Bad Timing

Maybe I should not have called
To hear your voice once more
You sound just as angry
As you ever did before

I won't try and judge you
Everyone has their way
Everyone has their battles
That's eating them everyday

Maybe it's just bad timing
And your day is not going well
Maybe you're just lonely
And you're missing me like hell

I only hoped we could be friends
But I know it's a little hard
I guess we both been through to much
We are always standing guard
Maybe time will heal all wounds
And end the need to make a fuss
I will love you either way
I refuse to fight over silly things, I've gotten of that bus

Maybe it's just bad timing
And your day is not going well
Maybe you're just lonely
And you're missing me like hell

Tony Payne 2015-44

Don't wait Until Tomorrow

The bonfire it was burning, inside my aching soul
I've never been this lonely, I've never been this cold
I don't know what the matter is, I've never been this old

Seems everyone is angry, Most just complain and cry
No one as no time, And I don't know why
Some people give up living, long before they die

Why can't we just be grateful, for the little things we got
Why don't we just say thank you, for supper that's in the pot
We should all be using gratitude, before our souls turn to friggin rot

Don't wait until tomorrow, you have to live your today
The longer we put off until tomorrow, the less rewards it will ever pay

We can all be happy, just you smile and see
When I look in to the mirror, I hope he smiles back at me
No need to live inside a prison, when you have a key

Don't wait until tomorrow, you have to live your life today
The longer we put off for tomorrow, the less rewards it will ever pay

Tony Payne 2015-45

Every Time It Rains

The front yard is looking beautiful
The painting is almost done
My life can't get any better
The kids are having fun

I gave up stressing about things
That I have no control
I gave up the whiskey
It was making me feel old

But I worry if the house will leak
Every time It rains
I worry about you baby
I hope you have no pain

I will soon be turning fifty
I have a full head of hair
I don't enjoy hangovers much
And I don't really like the beer

You say you were out fishing
I'm glad you take that in
You were always so afraid
To go out in boat way back when

But I worry if the house will leak
Every time It rains
I worry about you baby
I hope you have no pain

Tony Payne 2015-46

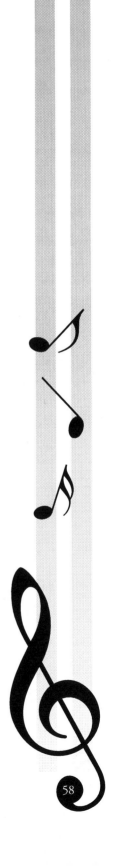

58

Smiley

Smiley is a wooden fisherman
That stands out by my door
He just stares out at the fishing boats
That are moored right of shore

All he ever thinks about
Is going out to sea
He will never find contentment
Being a carpenter like me

Smiley is a wooden fisherman
That stands out by my door
He just stares out at the fishing boats
That are moored right of shore

He was never happy
I see it in his one good eye
Sometimes when the sea gets rough
I think I hear him cry
I wish I had the power
To give him a joyous life
When he returns from his fishing boat
To his kids and loving wife

Smiley is a wooden fisherman
That stands out by my door
He just stares out at the fishing boats
That are moored right of shore

He never ever talks to me
To tell me he is ok
I don't think he really understands
Why things have to be this way

All he ever does
Is stand out there in the sun
His skin is turning rough and black
Just like every other fisherman

Smiley is a wooden fisherman
That stands out by my door
He just stares out at the fishing boats
That are moored right of shore

Tony Payne 2015-47

Lost love

I lay here and watch you sleeping
You look so content
How did we get so lonely
Like our money our love is spent

I reach down and caress you
That used to make you sigh
If only I could turn back time
I wouldn't see a tear fall from your eye

You used to love me beside you
We used to feel one and the same
It don't feel right to touch you
You never scream my name

We couldn't wait to make love
Now it is such a chore
I guess we still have the same animal desires
But we never ask for more
When it all is over
We just turn away
I can hear you crying
And my heart it melts like clay

In the morning we don't even speak
Both our hearts are cold
We know it's time to move on
Find ourselves before we both grow old

Tony Payne / 1015-48

Let go

Baby I'm sitting here thinking
How come we are just getting by
I always thought our love was forever
Now seem all we do is try

All this time we've been together
You never ask that much of me
I know we're not in love anymore
Why don't we just set us free

I hope the words we said can be forgiven
And we forgive everything we did
I know I often hurt you in anger
With words I should never have said

You know I'm not a hateful person
God only knows where I would be
If you never held onto my heart
At least love I had a chance to see
I guess we both are guilty
And we lived in a prison way too long
We both had our share of heartaches
I like to think it has made us strong

I have all kinds of love inside my heart
And I only have one plea
Sometimes we hang on to long
Let's let go of love that can never be

Tony Payne / 2015-49

No One Shoots Pool Any More

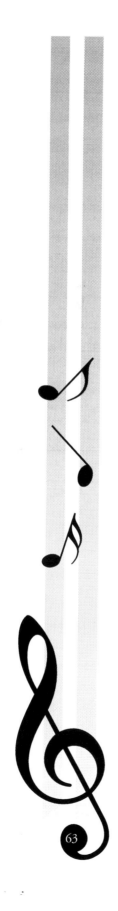

The bars they are all empty
Not like it used to be
No one shoots pool anymore
With old drunks like me
Sometimes I have to wonder
If people can really see
No one knows I think
What it means to be set free

We`re all tied to earthly positions
With money we haven't got
We are supposed to live in abundance
But give up on our want
Seems there is no love in our hearts
Our morals are all shot
We would sell our own soul
To look the richest of the lot

We really need to say thankyou
For what we have in this life
Think of your friendly neighbour
And never lust for his lovely wife
We are all so god damned greedy
It cuts just like a knife
We all want true happiness
Learn to play the guitar, drums and fife

The bars they are all empty
Not like they used to be
No one shoots pool anymore
With old drunks like me.

Tony Payne 2015-50

63

Back To Hell

I look up at the starry night
As I sit here all alone
With no more desire of getting drunk
And no need of getting stoned

Where I end up in this life
Time alone will tell
But where my mind as taken me before
I'm not going back to hell

I've lived a life of terrible ways
Drunken nights and frigged up days
I thought too much when I was alone
Thought I was happy, but I was stoned

I have always felt the hardships
Never knowing what to do
Always angry at myself
But always blaming you
I ask you for forgiveness
Most people will set me free
But the most difficult time I ever have
Is me forgiving me

Where I end up in this life
Time alone will tell
But where my mind as taken me before
I'm not going back to hell

Tony PAYNE/2015-51

How the Time Flies By

Everything changes, everyone knows
You can't keep on wearing that worn out clothes
Stop worrying about people that look down their nose
Oh how the time flies by

Old lovers never forget the past
True love is something that last
Time to slow down, we are all living to fast
Oh how the time flies by

Who do you see when you look in the glass
Do you recognise those eyes
Or is it a stranger from a long time ago
And do they still shed a tear when you cry

Don't ever let people, drag you down in the dirt
When you don't play the games they play, it`ll never hurt
Sometimes people just want to flirt
Oh how the time flies by
Sometimes people they never grow old
They find a true love that's meant to be
Often times they die, and are never told
They are not blind, but still can't see

Everything changes everyone knows
Make sure you're happy, it always shows
Find yourself shelter,
Where the warm wind blows

Oh how the time flies by
Oh how the time flies by
Oh how the time flies by

Tony Payne 2015-52

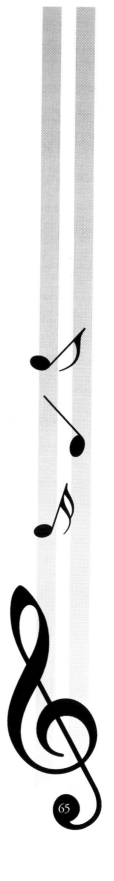

65

Fridays I Don't Even Try

Most days I fight to get you out of my mind
Baby I ain`t going to lie
Six days a week, I struggle holding back tears
Fridays I don't even try

When the whiskey starts working, and I come undone
Sometimes I wish I would die
I stay away from the bottle most of the time
But Fridays I don't even try

You know that I need you when I see your face
I know that you don't need to ask why
When light turns to darkness I put your pictures away
But Fridays I don't even try

24 hours a day, I'm thinking of you
Makes me wonder how I ever get by
I have to stop watching the clock on the wall
Fridays I don't even try
Baby I need you when you`re not around
Most time I do miss your sigh
I work some long hours, so your memory don't come around
But Fridays I don't even try

Most days I fight to get you out of my mind
Baby I ain`t going to lie
Six days a week, I struggle holding back tears
Fridays I don't even try
No, Fridays I don't even try

Tony Payne 2015-53

Brothers

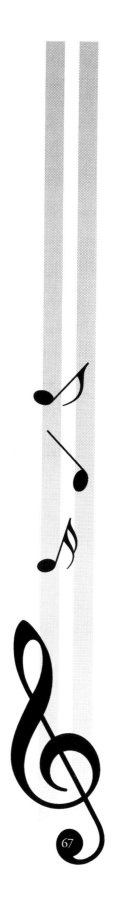

Brothers take great care of you
Pick you up when you`re feeling blue
Break your toys when they are new
They love you like no other

I remember when he held my hand
Built some dinky tracks in the sand
Protected me from that strange man
When all I wanted was a drink

You bought me my first beer
Gave me a condom when needed there
Bailed me out when it was clear
I would have lost the fight anyway

Gave me money when I was stuck
Forgave me when I wrecked your truck
Praised me up when I had bad luck
And he cried when I left home

Now I'm older I know for sure
When I'm gone he will miss me more
No more picking me up off the floor
When I'm too drunk to walk

Brothers take great care of you
Pick you up when you`re feeling blue
Break your toys when they are new
They love you like no other

Tony Payne 2015-54

On A Divided Highway

On a divided highway, just outside of town
I was driving really fast, not a soul around
Then I saw a girl, hitching for a ride
I stopped my van, unlocked the door, and she got inside

I asked her what she was doing, out there in the cold
She said "I don't know, I'm just getting old"
I said "can't you do that in a warmer place than this"
That's when I saw a smile, I'm glad I never missed

She looked so damn pretty, there was a twinkle in her eye
I asked if she would like a tea, and she began to cry
I asked what she doing out there all alone
"I used to have some so called friends, they just got me stoned"

I handed her my thermos, her hands they were like ice
She asked me what I wanted, for treating her so nice
My voice it sort of quivered, trying to be honest with my heart
I've been there before my love, everyone deserves another start

On a divided highway, I saw her fear just melt away
She showed me she was thankful, without a word to say
I just drove on slowly, and she just drank her tea
She suddenly turned and said, "no one rides for free"

She wondered if I had a place, where she could lay her head
I took her to my bayside home, and I laid her in my bed
She told me I could join her, I found her real hard to resist
As I headed for the couch, I knew that would be best

I woke up in the morning, she was sitting by my side
She kissed me on the cheek, tears fell from her eyes
She said "I'm heading home, to start my life again"
And I will never forget, how you helped me through my pain

On the divided highway, that led me out of town
I met up with the sweetest thing, which brought my heart around
She asked me what I wanted, and if it had a cost
She taught me to be honest, and I found my heart that I had lost

I was sitting at a fire, all alone there on the beach
I could feel someone was near me, but not within my reach
I finally found contentment, and wasn't feeling that much older
I was dreaming of those lovely eyes, when I felt a hand upon my shoulder

She ask if she could join me, I said it would make me proud
All of the feelings inside of me, were shouting right out loud
She sat down there beside me, oh man she held my hand
She said she can't forget the night, I changed her life there in my van

On a divided highway, was it faith or was it chance
I was driving really fast, thinking this was my last dance
She didn't even want a ride, she was looking for a hole
When the sun rises tomorrow, we will have each other's soul.

Tony H. Payne 2015- 55

Printed in the United States
By Bookmasters